WHY ANANSI HAS EIGHT THIN LEGS

by Jessica Lee Anderson
Illustrations by Marc Mones

Anansi the spider has eight fat legs.
Anansi is smart. He is also greedy!
One day Anansi takes a walk.
He smells peas.

Rabbit has a pot of peas.
"Smells good," said Anansi.
"Help me cook. Then you can have some,"
Rabbit said.

"I'm on a walk," Anansi said.
"I can't help. But I will help later."

He spins a web. He ties one end to his leg.
He ties the other end to the pot.

"Pull my web when it's time to stir.
Then I will come and help," said Anansi.

But he doesn't plan to help.
He plans to take the peas and run!

Anansi walks on.
Soon he smells beans.
Monkey has a pot of beans.

"Help me cook. Then you can have some,"
Monkey said.

"I will help later," said Anansi.

Then Anansi ties a web from his leg
to the pot.

"Pull this when it's time to stir.
I will come and help," he said.
He doesn't plan to help!

Anansi walks on.
He sees six more friends.
Each friend cooks something.

So Anansi ties webs to their pots, too.

Now he has a web on each leg!

It's time to stir the pots.
Each friend pulls on one web.
Each web pulls on one of Anansi's legs.
Soon his eight fat legs grow thin.

The webs snap!
Now Anansi has thin legs.
And this is why spiders have thin legs.